Kisses

in

the

Raw

Night

Victoria Garton

P   O   E   M   S

BkMk Press
College of Arts & Sciences

University of Missouri-Kansas City
5216 Rockhill Rd., Rm. 204
Kansas City, MO 64110-2499

ACKNOWLEDGMENTS

Certain of these poems have previously appeared in the following publications: *Prairie Schooner, The Chariton Review, Kansas Quarterly, Concerning Western Poetry, Missouri Philological Association Publications, Missouri Poets: An Anthology, Southern Poetry Review, Aldebaran, The COE Review, Orphic Lute, The New Delta Review, Farmer's Market, The Nebraska Review, Bogg Magazine, Anthology of Missouri Women Writers.*

Illustrations & design assistance by Robin Gale Jaffe.
Jacket and book design by Michael Annis.
Typography by Michael Annis/Typography.
Printing by Inter-Collegiate Press, Shawnee Mission, Kansas.

Library of Congress Cataloging-in-Publication Data
Garton, Victoria.
   Kisses in the Raw Night.

   I. Title
PS3557.A797K57   1989   811'.54   88-19310
ISBN 0-933532-69-5

BkMk Press — UMKC

Dan Jaffe, Director
Ben Furnish, Associate Editor

Here are boxes of poems,
like decorative antique boxes within boxes.
Here are *"The Music Box,"*
"Pandora's Box," "The Story Box," "The Innermost Box,"
and also *"The Souvenir Box"* of foil, and hearts,
kept tucked away on some high
shelf after all is done.

Victoria Garton wrote these poems between 1978 and 1987 while she was
living in southwestern Missouri and serving as the first woman county
commissioner in Vernon County. Her poetry has appeared in *Prairie
Schooner, The Chariton Review, Kansas Quarterly, Southern Poetry Review,* and
other journals and literary magazines. She has worked as an artist-in-
education through the Missouri Arts Council. She is currently a supervisor
with the Missouri Department of Elementary and Secondary Education in
Jefferson City, Missouri.

Contents

*This book is dedicated to my husband, Norman,
and to my sons, George and John.*

THE MUSIC BOX

The Flute Speaks

For a pointed tongue
and breath hot
against my cold metal
I will lift snakes
upon tail tips,
spin turtles on their shells,
marshal the toads
in their warty coats,
till fish mouth their secrets.

If you carry me
on your last breath,
I will crescendo
in a flurry of charging notes,
then lie
with your fingerprints
in a bed of velvet
echoing fertile songs
through my chambers.

Spring Song

Honeysuckling off the piney ridge,
yeasty as evening
rising out of the valley,
the siren's call is honed
as the fiddle's cut,
lush as mountain laurel.

Schooled in the soured-sweat taste
of honeysuckle honey,
the mountain boys swarm.
They are the sons of toothless men
who halt their whittling, grin,
and lick winter-parched lips.

Because You Are Different There is Mystery

My fellow traveler into the infinite,
do not write too often, and do not display
all the bumps and blemishes of your every day,
and if love can celebrate illusion, let it.

Where is the rub when we so often match wits?
When sands in an hourglass must always blend,
they lose their rough edges and recommend
a shorter time for the passing of their minutes.

We need to stretch the mystery in time's element.
Dear man, be crystallized so different
that only dreamy distance dare complement
the grating moments of our entanglement.

Kisses in the Raw Night

In the raw night
I swallow your kisses
like meaty oysters,
yet our skins peel apart
opening wounds,
salt licks for the wind.

Shucked, I go off
while my tongue,
restless as a beached oysterman,
searches my mouth
for a seed,
a grain of sand to rub against.

Sea Song

Let us look
to the sea
for love.
In buoyancy
let us be
light and reversible.
In love
let us be
pure.
If on this earth
we must be
separate, let us return
to cradling water.
In the sea
of love's quick,
slippery moment,
let us be
one.

Love, Hot as the Mustard Moon

A dog barks and our love
turns the moon to mustard.
How is it a dog is always barking
as the world ends?

We gallop naked,
ride to the end of our nerves,
become the purple clouds
nibbling the spicy moon.

All the while,
a dog is barking,
howling us down
to the warming earth.

Poem to a Letter

Waiting for you I am unblessed.
A stone with no singing soul.
A reptile heart hardly pumping blood.
A brook under snow. I am a bear
sleeping it out in winter's cave.

I approach that oasis, my mailbox,
knowing thirst, knowing how far
the desert stretches before the lost.
I swear the mailbox throbs.

Then you sizzle in my hands
and I enter the sphere of your words;
those blood donors, those songs.

Drawing Out Heat

"And he came face to face with the paradox,
a woman hot and cold."

He is small now,
boyish in his nakedness.
He jumps in and out
of a suspended marionette,
earning her laughter.

She lies on the sheet in honeyed light.
Her hand on her skin
is a honey stick
drawing out heat.

He could pant again blowing the coals,
but she has curled for sleep
like a pampered, milk-fed cat.
She will awaken when morning enters.

There is no laughter
from the iced man
staring back from the mirror.
He quickly steps into his pants,
shivers as he dresses.

The Oyster Speaks

Sometimes
you surprise,
tossing and churning.
Too often
you are the enemy
against whom I close
fastening myself
to a rock.

When Neptune
leaves with your thunder,
I send out small feelers,
slowly offer
fold after fold.
At times
I am open,
letting you enter.

But even when caught
in your lapping attention,
I cling
to what is more solid
than you who might plant
a grain of sand,
or drop me
on a moon-swept beach.

Round Dancing at the Community Center

I follow the widow who goes *front to front*
with the balding man. All day
on the production line she puts the folds
of a bat's wing into strips of black vinyl.
The days are no different from the days
she put folds into diapers. Her children grown,
she comes from her empty rooms and I come
with my husband. Forty of us come
bringing weariness,
long faces from the long day of work.

At the caller's insistence, we *acknowledge*
and *part*. Then it's *half-vine, two by two,*
and *swing*, chest to breast. Passing
from man to man, I begin to dream encounters.
I am spun by fathers, brothers,
and finger-squeezing lovers. Giddy as tops,
we plump and slender women spin
and giggle as boots stray between our legs
and men so near grow red.

I am years younger when, *semi-close* and *touch*,
my husband comes awkward and breathless
from the perfumed embraces and sweatered nipples
which were his for an instant.
Holding hands we giggle and swing and turn,
singing the steps, ready to dance off again.

Voices From Under the Rock

Prologue

There is a voice which speaks to man.
It is a slow, low voice.
Out of suck and pull of mud,
out of night's furry darkness,
out of an ear's wax —
the voice.

I have heard it deep in water,
even in the tomb.
It is the sound of the dead
as earth mothers them down,
the assurance in shovel on shovel
of dirt, the sound
of earth easing death down.

First Voice

To beaver, bear, and beast
the voice is wood, honey, flesh.
To muskrat the voice
is a home of mud.
To man a place to come to.
The voice says, "Rub, rub,"
lays him down,
cradles him, is a cave
where swaddled in darkness
his face is licked
by the drip off rock.

Thick on tongue, the voice
is milk, amniotic fluid, salt.

Croons, "Never leave,
never leave."

Second Voice

Mew, Mew.
The milk-fed cat,
the thick-fleshed cat
lies on the belly
of the man,
purrs forth the dream
of thorned footpads
on spine.
Does tricks
when she's caught,
when she's played the game,
been captured,
caressed.
The voice is the mew,
"I have you,
I have you."

Third Voice

The voice of whiteness
comes out of a shell,
out of a lily's Easter throat,
out of dew on the whitest rose.

The voice is nurse, bride,
gull swinging out
over an ocean's white tips.
The voice is light,

mother's pillow
of breast.

Yet it tastes of ash,
a bracing Seltzer of ash.
Death Angel.
An edible dream.
Eat and be filled.
Lie down and sleep.

Fourth Voice

Out of mist,
out of smoke,
out of steam,
out of sun wavering
over snow —
the voice.
Its message
beyond chime of bell,
beyond music.
The marble hand made flesh.
It reaches
out of flaw, wound, and wrinkle,
past scar, crevice, and chasm.
It reaches
into the womb
to lead you up
out of ash of dream,
out of ash of
all you were
and never were.

Chorus

All those voices
you found
when you lifted the mushroom's cap,
when you opened the oyster's shell. . . .

Blessed chorus.
Mother, lover, virgin, saint.
Let the chorus diminish
wave on wave.
Death mother you are found out.
Sweet woman you are found.

PANDORA'S BOX

With Intimacy the Myth

With intimacy the myth
I wanted to believe,
I planted honeysuckle
by the chimney.

His job was to stand,
and hers to stretch
and twist
and cling to brick.

It's tough being counselor
to chimney and honeysuckle,
pruning and tying
season after season.

It's no secret
she tosses her leaves,
sprawls in the sun with grass.
And old brick-face
busy with his smoke
is hot only when she's dormant.

But once a spring
he warms a chill
while she stirs some green,
and yellow-orange wisps of flame
are the risks they take
to mingle pungent scent
and smoke.

Jack Frost's Bride

Deep in anthracitic regions
I wear black lace.
Touch me.
My skin holds the deepest chill of winter.

I am miles below love,
like the once-living leaf
learning the density of humus.
Almost tongue-tied I ask.

I am compressed coal,
learning striations of earth.
Bring the spades of your fingers.
Bring a pick.

Jack Frost's bride waits
for a miner's swing,
for a plucker of seams.
Oh let me go loose into spring.

The Pumpkin Eater's Shut-In

Like a promise of lichen
pumpkin vines go flowering
out past the boundaries
of the fence,
past its shadow of doubt.

Well, Peter, old spouse,
how green you've grown
hugging one orange dream.
Cream and sugar
offer easy redemption,
at least to a pumpkin.

In Nutmeg and Cinnamon
I might have kissed
your green-veined hands.
From any Mecca
I might have returned
as a wife.

But you took my hoe
when I straddled it,
took the seeds
I wore for pearls,

took each vine back
to the fence saying,
"I keep her.
I keep her very well."

Doorkeeper,
you do not guess
the lushness of a shell.
These nodules
on my rooted eyes are dreams.
Shut in I have traveled deep
into this womb
where I keep myself.

Nothing Personal

You didn't know his name
was Rumpelstiltskin,
when he jumped from behind straw.
The gold he spun was honey
sucked from your own lips.
What could you do, you two alone
in a locked room?
It was nothing personal.

That night the wicked witch
grew in your mother's reflection.
The next morning your mirror
was broken and you were
the bitten apple. The worst rapist
is the wizened dwarf you assume
is neuter.
Your mistake is nothing personal.

From stone cottage you watch
as unencumbered sisters go off
to dance. While you write, poems
turn to frogs. You sleep as under

a step-mother's curse until, swollen
as the pumpkin in which you
didn't leave, you swear off glass dreams.
It becomes personal.

After that, you don't need
magic men or a someday prince.
You stand up and scream,
"I never asked for this."
When he whispers, "A woman always does,"
you hang his rumpled skin.

Boughten Rooms

A man, a woman, and a boughten room.
Things are kept back when we pay to enter.
The secrets stay behind the empty walls.
The place beyond the bridge in the cheap print
is not accessible.

Who thinks of such things? He punches
the pillow which has cushioned so many.
Smokes. Tomorrow morning
his mouth will taste of old tobacco.

She asks nothing of the room. Does not
move a chair or realign a picture.
This is one of those places where nobody lives.
Of him she asks only that he follow
like a dog on scent.

Real love too difficult, they go
through the motions. The bed moans old stories.
He says words which are not his, which
in lieu of love she takes for small payment.

Next morning,
pretending that they crossed the bridge,
they politely reminisce about the place beyond.
Having invested little, they leave things
of no value, a piece of foil, a tray of ashes,
a slip of crumpled paper.

Totaled

New I was fully equipped and chosen
for my padded dash and big spare tire.
A fifties trapping of success,
a honey in tantalizing turquoise,
or fresh pink, I carried
the burden of a man and cushioned
his weary limbs homeward.
On weekends he caressed my surface,
patted my backside when friends came,
and bragged about what I could do.

Later there were children spilling
out my doors and my tires were always
threadbare. When I was finally brought
to this patch of weeds, I was ready
for a life of my own. Still they came
ravaging my spare parts, and
the sun peeled away that brighter me,
and gravity came with his intimate touch
bringing me down to my axles.

THE STORY BOX

Marriage Miracle

On imprints of hooves frozen into ground
gone white in the headlights of a truck,
she follows the man whose work
is the birth and death of animals.

Tripping, she feels the unsteady aisle
where she had walked to meet him,
awkward as the heifer ahead straining with calf.
She hears again her father's bitten-back sobs.

The cow, kneeling with belly to cold earth,
goes down with a crack of bones.
They had knelt on a rail for prayer
through the everlasting notes of "Our Father."

He had crouched then, as now over the steam
of uterus and a bluish hoof came new to air,
and teetered on trembling sound.
Always she felt in her knees that tremble.

The places a man is called to in the night
are not the promised honeymoon places.
There was a ring between them, bright

as the one on chains he pulls from sudsy water.

Into harness of steel he hooks the ring,
then circles legs with links of metal, and braces
for the ratcheted pull against nature and womb.
She had been a child when he took her.

He stops, loosens the chains, shoves
the head back into the blood girdle. Shoulder
heaving for the right turn, the angle of exit,
he works the brute forces of birth.

In their marriage bed, she knows the pull
of those arms. The calf lumbers out
onto winter ground, is lifted and dropped
until it chokes for breath in the powdery light.

With burlap sack she wipes off mucus,
then moves aside as the calf saws and wobbles
and like their marriage finally stands, a thing apart.
As he cleans his hands, she whispers, "Miracle."

At the Playground

She hesitated, considered her coat,
ran a hand over the black plastic seat,
sat and pumped until she was flying.
He stood stiffly, watching
the girl in her come and go,
heard her voice full of laughter.

Long ago she had written a story
of a brother, a cousin, and a swing.
She rose toward it now.
Her seventh grade words like her legs
had been awkward but the story,
the story had lived and was floating
out where she could almost reach.

Giving no warning she jumped, ran a few steps,
recovered herself. Even if she had yelled,
he could not have caught her.
"It's getting colder," he said.
He could not have caught her
because the girl in her was a story
he could not read. Behind him
the quiet woman smoothing her coat
lagged like an emptied swing.

Alone Together

He crosses the thatch of old stalks
leaving her alone where the creek
breaks the flow of sunlight
and a short fall of water
pours from an earthen pitcher.

Earlier, he might have waited,
woven her hand into his
and led her to a quick romp
on the winter-weary grass.
Earlier, they might have sat
over the creek on extended sandstone
and a single bird's call might have opened the air
and let them through.

But they never lived that sundog love
and now he walks ahead
and she moves in a later time
when alone she will pause
where a creek breaks the flow of sunlight.
She will remember this time
they do not share
as a time they were together.

Waiting for the Ducks

They were only waiting for the ducks
to swim across to them.
Not gamblers waiting for horses
or dice or lucky cards,
not dreamers waiting for ships
to come in,
just two people filling the time
between work and dinner.

Yet somehow it seemed
that if only the wind would change,
if only the sun would hang on,
if only the water would calm,
then maybe the ducks,
the beautiful green-headed ducks,
would swim across to them.

Meeting in the Off-Season

It was one of those fall mornings
in the Ozarks,
the hard maples had gone soft, melted
into russet. I had nothing to do.

You came walking through fallen leaves.
Like a lover delivered by a dream, but
we had nothing to say.

All morning the drone of a vacuum herding the
oak leaves freed us from talk.
We stood apart and watched the lake
chew the limestone embankment.

I chewed the soft skin of my cheek,
tasted the nightmare of love's off-season.

Danger Zone

So we have reached
the high cliff
from which love soars or falls.
The path back is a tangle of thorns.
I pull my hands away.
My voice says, "Fly,"
yet every impulse
demands the brittle snap of bones.

A Civilization Ends

I.

In this home, this minor civilization,
at my grandfather's table of oak,
at his grandfather's table of walnut,
we are sorting the silver,
and packing the linens, the towels,
and the pans.

There is a new weight on us,
the shadows of the chandelier
grow heavy, sink in,
like our break with the past.
How we have struggled in this house
to keep dinner at six,
to welcome each holiday,
to solidify an "us" through habits.

I am ready to sell the television,
some chairs, a bed, a sweeper,
the holiday ornaments. Things,
mere things. But am I ready
to hang "us" up like some limp apron?

II.

What if I straighten the covers,
press the napkins, pay the bills, dust
off the wedding certificate?
Our family portraits are askew,
the floor is aslant, the foundation weak.
Grandmother's dish has a crack.
Is it too late when all the proper ways
of blessing food and getting up and
saying please, all the niceties are gone?
Where did we lose the habit of love?

Opening the Envelope

She opens the envelope
of herself
and what she finds
is not junk mail, nor a chain letter,
nor anything expected
like "Dear Occupant."

What she finds
is a bit threatening
like a "payment due,"
but due to herself.

What she finds
is a long letter
still being written
by someone
she was beginning to forget.

THE INNERMOST BOX

Adam and the Ribmate

He preferred solitude,
the garden of God's creation, himself,
and since he did not like strangers,
was glad God had limited creation.

She wanted company so much
she talked to the snake
and having come from a borrowed rib
thought nothing of borrowing
from the tree of knowledge.

They were the original pair
and parented a race
of those who do not want
to end up at odds but do
and those who bite into life
to get love pains,
stomach pains,
birth pains.

The Wall, Pyramus, and Thisbe

Is it fair that the mulberry
took the color of their blood
and stands as a seasonal memory?
The white mulberry, anemic
as young love, took a healthy color
from all that sentiment;
and ever since Pyramus and Thisbe
gushed blood and words, the mulberry
has drawn lovers like flies.

What of me, the wall between
their houses? How many lovers
still stand with noses pressed
passionately kissing a wall and
whispering through chinks?
Oh for the bygone days when a wall
filtered promises and absorbed
kisses. Had these lovers
not seen lions and jumped
to conclusions, they might have lived
to value walls if only for the joy
of tearing them down.

Claudia and Max

Since Claudia the wife
and Max the coroner
have taken up bird watching,
life is a Lark
on the telephone wires,
a Finch in the eaves.
But is it a Finch
or is Max flinching again?
Oh for life as a grand affair
with one's spouse.
Wasn't that the reason
for the counselor?

We will leave behind
the body of the marriage.
Pretend it's at the morgue,
pretend it's a corpse, silent
as Max is.

We will enter the woods,
the leafy silence, where
Claudia watches Max
with his thirty-dollar bird books,

his high-powered binoculars.
If bird watching were not
a silent sport, she would proclaim
the good time they are having.

Meanwhile,
Max considers his investments
and watches (like the counselor did)
the intimate habits
of birds on weak twigs
watching themselves being watched.

Circe and Odysseus

Her Story:

Independent as a thistle, I took
nothing but color from the sunset,
never thought there was an equation
to be completed. Yes,
I turned his men to swine, but
I was no swineherd, needed
no man to provide function.
Does a goddess need a job description?
I was a thistle, rigidly majestic,
then I was a plucked bloom
in Odysseus's bouquet.
Shall I curse Hermes magic plant?
No, this story grows in love's garden.
I'll implicate my woman's heart.

His Story:

Men should wander, wage war,
come home to murder and mayhem.
Circe was my truest danger.
Never in the dark years lost
to Calypso did I lose the far vision.
In the frightful night of Polyphemus,
I blinded the obvious eye of evil.
I was not caught unbound when sirens
sang, but by the insidious thorns
of a woman subdued. She was

47

an entangling vine to my oak
and fed me bitter acorns
she called sweet kisses.

In the Counselor's Opinion:

They were happy for a year.
He conquered her with force and cunning.
She conquered him with acquiescence.
His roots were loosened but kept their hold;
her thorns grew dull but remained thorns.

In my utilitarian view there is nothing to save
except Hermes' milky flower of black root,
which grows in the myth of romance and
deadens the pain of love.

_____ THE SOUVENIR BOX

Remember the Girl

Remember the girl who saw stars
cut the velvet night? Remember
how she burned with the fireflies,
how her voice sang the joy
of the freed cicada?

There was dew on the lips
of all she loved; and love
touched even the nested birds, the owl
kneading the night with his wings,
the mother-of-pearl moon.

Do not look for her now
in the hiding place of the cricket. Turn
from her face in the bat's narrowing circle,
for her heart is surely a whetstone
where the years have sharpened the stars.

The Lover Inside

The lover inside picks mushrooms
from an ever fertile place
and lays then on the salad,
though the woman knows that her husband
will brush away these tokens,
take what he needs from the breast of veal,
scrape the parsley from the potatoes,
suck the thinly sliced lemon, eating it out
like the cherries from the crust
and then belching
turn from her to his couch.

Later at the sink,
stabbing the soapsuds, the wife
assigns the first death
not to her husband
but to the lover
who rolled the plump lemons,
touched her breasts,
and sliced the mushrooms.

Wake for Our Dead Love

I sat all night at the wake
for our dead love.
You were not invited,
yet our song came in
unexpected as the roses
you never sent. Overwrought,
I shoved the nickelodeon
away from the wall, removed
that record, and cracked it
over the skull
of our dear departed.

Sugared memories
lay in crumbles
and I sat for the next
stage.
Love is a needle
in a deepening groove.
Our song played again
and again.

Lament for a Defective Heart

A woman will give far too much of herself.
I know this. That is why I read feminist tracts
and talk against the enemy.
But why was I given this defective heart,
the one which shapes my days like so much clay
around your over-riding image?
Oh for five minutes of pure objectivity.
I need to see the human hiding in the dream;
to be clean and fierce, an Amazon
armored for war against irrational love.

Dead Letters

I have put all of your old letters
in the pit for dead flowers
at the cemetery. The post office
will not take them back. Neither
will the post office change my address
unless I move. Therefore,
I have received yet another
loveless letter from you.

I did not invite this,
would not have broken the seal
had you not scribbled my name
in hieroglyphics. "Drop by anytime,"
is the memorable last line
of your unwanted letter which
I have tacked up at the post office
by the posters of other bad hombres.

Why don't you drop by
the pit of dead flowers at the cemetery
and read again those old soggy words?

Husband's Lament

Oh, will she on the day
I'm gone
regret her aproned efficiency,
the way she plumped me up
like an old pillow gone lumpy?

Oh, will she on the day
I'm gone
remember all that I brought her
along with the dust of the world?

Oh, will she on the day
I'm gone
turn her microscopic view
from droppings, crumbs, and litter?

Or, will she on the day
I'm gone
sail forth smelling of lemon
to gather the last clipped whiskers
and flush me out of her life?

The Last Time

New grass up through the old
urged us to some decision.
Our commitments moved
in slow motion, harried players.
Those other lives tangled our limbs.
We moved without freedom,
without joy.

How could we bear
spring's green insistence?

Had we known this ending in winter,
we might have held on.

Getting Hold of Yourself

Is not as simple as
slipping a hand around your shoulder
or stuffing yourself under your arm
and trotting on home.

You are like a compass
trying to get a hold on true north.
Your friends can not edge you
into a convenient slot or ease
you through the wicket
though they will try.

There is little you can do
but wait to settle. Wait
as the perimeters shrivel
and the directions you
go off into convolute.
Crazy whims like relatives
finally congregate.

What you can do is mosey around
until you find a self
with the jaw of Churchill
and the heart of Margaret Thatcher.
And don't look too cagey
when you offer your arm.

Passion and After

1.

In the sudden smell of sulphur
you feel dizzy. Love takes off the top
of your head quick as a flame
takes off the top of a match.

Wide and flaring, you warm
all those unexpected things;
the song birds under the eave,
small creatures under the grass.

What is close at hand comes
to you in an orange glow.

2.

When passion begins to die
it is the slow death of a candle,
the wick's habit eating away the wick.

The life that moved in the flame,
that danced with heart's strings, blurs.
A hiss like fear beats down the flame,
makes it jumpy as a captured heart,
sad as a singed wing beating out a circle.

Too close to the fire for too long,
nerve ends wax over. You move closer.

3.

Later, when you remember that love,
you see again the candle, its tall self.
You see all that was lost in the melting.
It is then your eyes wax over
and the close joys of your kindled heart
slip back undercover.

Ash on your tongue, you put aside fire,
go out to the cold world in your old coat,
give yourself up to the hurry hum-drum.

Shut the Door

Shut the door on all the ladies
with their cakes.
Say no thanks to hugs and kisses
and to lovers with arms extended.
Shut away the adjusting, insecure
half self.

Take a blessing from the rain.
Let heavy leaves be poultice.
If you are not healed
when the world returns, howl.
Be the indignant dog
wrenched from shattered sleep.

She Loves as She Can

What you need you already have
accounted for like hairs on the head.
To live on this earth requires love,
the kind that gets watered and fed
with daily solitude. The seeds
squirreled away, the winter store,
the harvest carefully sorted from weeds,
the remembered deed, remembered chore;
all the ordered gatherings
will not keep wind from thinning your hair
or keep you safe on capricious wings.
Nothing and everything is guaranteed. Fair
catch comes to the expectant fisherman,
also storms. Accepting, she loves as she can.

OTHER BOOKS FROM BkMk PRESS

Adirondack, poems by Roger Mitchell. "Mitchell patiently stands aside, to allow these Adirondack hills, forests and people to speak for themselves.... *Adirondack* is a fine example of style, or form, growing naturally out of its own material." *—Paul Metcalf.*
$8.95, 64 pages, cloth with jacket

Plumbers, poems by Robert Stewart. "These poems are moving, experienced, and, in their own hardbitten earthy way, pretty elegant. I love the way Stewart's affection for his subject, his genuine sweetness, keeps being close-shaved by a tough, realistic sense of limits. The knowledge in these poems is hard-won, the craft impressive." *—Phillip Lopate.*
$8.50, 64 pages, cloth with jacket

Press Box & City Room, columns by Peter L. Simpson & George Gurley. Two outspoken columnists reflect on everything from art to baseball, national politics to small town gossip. With wit and candor, they examine the ordinary as well as the peculiar.
$10.95, 120 pages, cloth with jacket

Time Winds, poems by Alfred Kisubi. Poems by a Ugandan poet reflecting the struggle for African identity under dictatorship and technology. "Clearly his poetry is in the tradition of ... distinguished voices such as those of Chinua Achebe, Wole Soyinka, Dennis Brutus and Okot P'Bitek." *—Andrew Salkey.*
$9.95, 80 pages, cloth with jacket

Tanks, short fiction by John Mort. "Chilling glimpses of the Vietnam War. These are terrifying, but sensitive stories." *—Bobbie Ann Mason.*
$8.95, 88 pages, paper

Selected Poems of Mbembe Milton Smith. "A brooding soul with a brilliant, searching consciousness." *—Cottonwood Review.* "One of our most nourishing poets ... He used language deftly with lively, affectionate respect." *—Gwendolyn Brooks.*
$8.95, 116 pages, paper

Seasons of the River, poems by Dan Jaffe, color photos by Bob Barrett. Prize-winning poems about the Missouri River accented with exceptional color photographs. "[These] poems are marked by strong, breathtaking beginnings and affirmative endings ... this is a book of timeless interest." *—St. Louis Post-Dispatch.*
$14.95, 64 pages, cloth (8½ x 11″)

Wild Bouquet, by Harry Martinson. The first American collection of these nature poems by the Swedish Nobel Laureate. Translated and with an introduction by William Jay Smith and Leif Sjöberg.
$10.95, 76 pages, cloth with jacket

Before the Light, poems by Ken Lauter. Three narratives probe the agonies of modern life: Lauter moves from the making of a porno "snuff" film to the murder of an adult retarded son to the making of the A-bomb.
$6.95, 52 pages, cloth

The Record-Breaking Heatwave, poems by Jeff Friedman. "This is urban poetry, working class poetry, strongly felt, carefully observed, cleanly written ..." *—Donald Justice.*
$6.95, 56 pages, cloth

To Veronica's New Lover, poems by Marc Monroe Dion. "Marc Dion has a reporter's eye for the telling detail, the poet's ear for the jammed vernacular ... full of booze, bitterness, and Irish machismo in neighborhoods 'pregnant and heavy-footed with life'." *—Peg Knoepfle.*
$7.95, 64 pages, cloth

The Woman in the Next Booth, poems by Jo McDougall. A native of the Arkansas Delta, Jo McDougall presents "the funk and smell of humanity," says Miller Williams. "Artful and serious work," comments Howard Nemerov.
$8.50, 64 pages, cloth with jacket

The Studs of McDonald County, poems by Joan Yeagley. "If there is a steel edge to these poems, there is a deep joy as well, something that comes when the place has been chosen and it is as rich and varied as the seasons." —*John Knoepfle*.

$6.95, 56 pages, cloth

The Eye of the Ghost: Vietnam Poems by Bill Bauer. "Bill Bauer takes us well into the experience of Vietnam with a sure sense of the catastrophe that war proved for those who were involved. These poems demonstrate not only craft and dedication to the poet's art, but also an abiding commitment to justice and compassion." —*Bruce Cutler*.

$7.95, 56 pages, cloth

Artificial Horizon, short fiction by Laurence Gonzales. "... a first rate young writer whose work merits attention from anyone seeking lively idiom, authentic detail and a fresh point of view ..." —*Edward Abbey*.

$8.95, 104 pages, paper

Missouri Short Fiction, edited by Conger Beasley, Jr. Twenty-three short stories by Missouri writers including Bob Shacochis, Speer Morgan, James McKinley, John Mort, Charles Hammer, David Ray and others.

$8.95, 176 pages, paper

The Hippopotamus: Selected Translations 1945-1985 by Charles Guenther. Poems translated from Eskimo, Greek, Hungarian, French, Italian, and Spanish. "A compact and elegant collection by an acknowledged master of the craft." —*Kansas City Star*.

$6.50, 76 pages, paper

Mbembe Milton Smith: Selected Poems. "A brooding soul with a brilliant, searching consciousness." —*Cottonwood Review*. "Mbembe was— IS— one of our most nourishing poets. He used language deftly, with lively, affectionate respect ... His legacy will continue to warm literature." —*Gwendolyn Brooks*.

$8.95, 116 pages, paper

In the Middle: Midwestern Women Poets, edited by Sylvia Griffith Wheeler. Poems and essays by Alberta Turner, Sonia Gernes, Diane Hueter, Janet Beeler Shaw, Patricia Hampl, Joan Yeagley, Cary Waterman, Roberta Hill Whiteman, Dorothy Selz, and Lisel Mueller.

$9.50, 120 pages, paper

Dark Fire by Bruce Cutler. A book length narrative poem exploring the restlessness of a fading flower child. "A lively, imaginative and finely crafted tale of modern life." — *Judson Jerome, Writers Digest*.

$5.25, 64 pages, paper

Selected Poems of John Knoepfle. "Among the finest work of our time." —*Abraxas*. "Contains poems that ought to become permanent parts of the American poetic tradition." —*Chicago*.

$6.50, 110 pages, paper

Writing in Winter by Constance Scheerer. Includes a rewrite of the Cinderella myth and tributes to Anne Sexton and Sylvia Plath. "One of the fresher voices out of the Midwest. Her portraits of what she has seen, felt and imagined are vivid and memorable." —*David Ray*.

$5.25, 80 pages, paper

Real & False Alarms by David Allan Evans. "This book will be remembered with critical acclaim ... it deserves the widest possible readership I can encourage." —*James Cox*, editor, *Midwest Book Review*.

$5.25, 64 pages, paper